Antonio Evaristo Morales-Pita, PhD has worked as a university professor for fifty-six years in Cuba, Mexico, and the USA, where he has been the recipient of numerous national awards. He has written and published sixteen books.

In the US, he self-published *Havana-Merida-Chicago (A Journey to Freedom)*, 2500 sold copies, and *Gladys, My Unforgettable Love*. Austin Macauley has published: *Is It Possible to Inspire Anyone? Is It Always Fun to Travel Abroad? Grit + Tenacity + Proactiveness: Pulling the Bull by the Horns, Havana-Merida-Chicago 2nd edition, Are You Ready to Improve Habits, May Empathy Lead to Sense of Purpose through Tenacity?, May Anyone Become a Better Human Being by Adopting the Hero Code?* and *Tenacity + Passion + Patience +Self-Rejection to Failure.*

Antonio is an inspirational speaker, promoting his books in colleges, universities, factories, and business firms. He has been an official contributor to newspapers, and journals. Antonio can speak, write, and read in Spanish, English, Russian, Italian and French.

In memoriam to my mother, Siria,
Who exerted a considerable influence on my pedagogic,
scientific, and writing career.
To the indelible remembrance of my wife, Gladys,
Who transmitted and made me learn the deep feeling of
empathy, in its deepest human meaning.
To my two children, Rosita and Tonito,
Whose lives and performances materialize my dreams and
aspirations as a father.

Antonio Evaristo
Morales-Pita, PhD

Is It Possible to Embrace Seniority with Optimism and Happiness?

AUSTIN MACAULEY PUBLISHERS™

LONDON • CAMBRIDGE • NEW YORK • SHARJAH

Ordering Information
Quantity sales: Special discounts are available on quantity purchases by corporations, associations, and others. For details, contact the publisher at the address below.

Publisher's Cataloging-in-Publication data
Morales-Pita, PhD, Antonio Evaristo
Is It Possible to Embrace Seniority with Optimism and Happiness?

ISBN 9798889104407 (Paperback)
ISBN 9798889104414 (ePub e-book)

Library of Congress Control Number: 2023921636

www.austinmacauley.com/us

First Published 2024
Austin Macauley Publishers LLC
40 Wall Street, 33rd Floor, Suite 3302
New York, NY 10005
USA

mail-usa@austinmacauley.com
+ 1 (646) 5125767

Table of Contents

Chapter I
Is It Possible to Embrace Seniority with Optimism and Happiness?

"To be optimistic is to assume things will work out. To be hopeful is to realize things can work out if you work at them. Hope requires responsibility and agency; optimism relieves us of both. In rooting for your sports team, choose optimism. In rooting for democracy, choose hope."

– Eric Liu

"Optimism doesn't mean that you are blind to the reality of the situation. It means that you remain motivated to seek a solution to whatever problems arise."

– The Dalai Lama

"I always like to look on the optimistic side of life, but I am realistic enough to know that life is a complex matter."

– Walt Disney

"Optimism is a happiness magnet. *If you stay positive, good things and good people will be drawn to you."*
– Mary Lou Retton

Definition of optimism

https://www.successwithcrm.com › blog › optimism-mean…

Optimism means embracing reality

You can accept that there will be bad days, but also good days. When you're grounded in reality, you know where you are and how far you need to go. Once you know how far your goal may be from where you are, optimism can give you the motivation to make plans to get to where you want to go.

How can I be more optimistic and happier? Surround yourself with positive people.

Identify the people in your life that you look up to for their optimism and spend more time with them. Observe the things they say, what they do, and what they choose not to do or say. You will notice patterns that you can adopt that will help you be more positive as well.

Optimists see life as one opportunity after another.

How you look at life can drastically affect how much you enjoy your life. Optimists expect the best out of life. If you were not raised with this attitude, take comfort: it can be learned.

Optimism is based on three basic tenets

According to Mary Kay Mueller in her book "Taking Care of Me: The Habits of Happiness":

1. Bad things do happen in life, but they are temporary.
2. Bad things in life are limited in scope and tend to be small or insignificant.
3. People have control over their environments.

Definition of optimism by Oxford Languages

Optimism is hopefulness and confidence about the future or the successful outcome of something.

Optimism is an attitude reflecting a belief or hope that the outcome of some specific endeavor, or outcomes in general, will be positive, favorable, and desirable. It involves believing that things will work out well, even in the face of adversity or challenges. *Wikipedia.*

This author's definition of embracing seniority with optimism and happiness comes from my late mother's behavior, which according to *Pedia.com* can be innate or learned. My mother was a tenacious fighter, ready to defeat procrastination, even though she ignored the word as such. For her, procrastination was a sort of hunch that might affect her in fulfilling a given task.

According to *https://www.mcleanhospital.org*, "one of the most common symptoms of procrastination is fear of a negative or unknown outcome. If you're fueled by anxiety, you may feel that you are inadequate, incapable, or a failure. You may put off tasks because you are afraid of not achieving "perfect" results. You may also fear being criticized."

Since my mother was almost illiterate until she turned 51, when she finished primary school, and nonetheless she was an inborn tenacious, it is interesting how inadvertently she could overcome procrastination because tenacity was in her genes.

Example No. 1. She asked me to interrupt my high school studies by learning English. Her motivation was the family's unfavorable financial situation, which required me to start working in a couple of years. She knew that I was an outstanding student in primary school and took it for granted that I could learn English quickly enough.

From the first chapter of my book *Grit + Tenacity + Proactivism*, I took two paragraphs that clearly exemplify how my mother, not only defeated procrastination but also taught me the same, although neither of us had any idea of that word.

She always supported me in the different studies I undertook. When I turned fourteen years old, I had finished secondary education and was getting ready to enter pre-college. She approached me and asked me to start studying English instead. The unusual change in my studies was due to the fact that my family needed me to financially contribute to maintain our home as soon as possible. Knowing English would allow me to start working as a bilingual secretary without having to wait for my graduation from a university. This was my first big educational challenge as a student because I only had rudimentary knowledge of the English language – as it was usually taught in grade school in Cuba. Studying as a full-time student would require a previous higher level of elementary English and a systematic dedication to the language for at least eight hours per day.

At this point, I should mention a circumstance that shows the impact my mother had on my student life. I was enrolled at the Havana Business Academy to Havana Business University in 2 years, which was widely known for its educational strictness in assigning students to different levels of English based on their level of vocabulary, grammar, reading, and writing skills. I had to do an exam on vocabulary. My level of preparation was so low that I had to guess on multiple-choice quizzes. I ignored most of the words, but I had a sort of guessing feeling that indicated to me which answers were right. As a result, I was placed at a level that was higher than the one I was really at. The academy principal was so surprised by my grade on the exam that she offered to my mother – who accompanied me in this adventure – the possibility of placing me in a lower level if I felt that level six was too high for me. The higher the initial level, the sooner I would finish my studies and that was in line with my mother's objectives. Therefore, she told the principal that she trusted in my academic capacity and intelligence. During the first two weeks the pressure was enormous on my brain – of course I did not know, then, that I would be facing harder challenges soon, and that this effort would prepare me – but I never gave up. Whenever I consulted my mother's opinion – when I resisted standing up after a fall – or when I felt overwhelmed by the number of difficult tasks I had undertaken, her answer was always, "Listen, my son, prepare your mind always to go ahead, never backward, You always must demand extra effort from yourself to grow and to succeed. Do not ever, ever, give up." As a result, I never felt defeated and always finished whatever I had started. What a way to positively influence my student life and performance!

After seventy years have gone by since the beginning of my learning English, it is clear to me which were the manifestations of tenacity, and the procrastinations that both of us defeated. The following table will help the readers to visualize the presence of procrastination and how it was defeated.

Table No 1:

Tenacious attitudes and procrastinating defeats in my early childhood.

Circumstance	Manifestation of tenacity	Overcoming procrastination
To be placed in English levels beyond Antonio's knowledge of the language	To accept the challenge of attempting vocabulary tests beyond a low English level.	Trying and succeeding to guess the unknown words pressed by my mother's pressure defeating the fear of doing poorly.
To be aware of the need to be placed in a high English level	To do the vocabulary test without fear of failure, trusting in innate reasoning and guessing skills.	To accept bravely to be placed in the sixth grade with an initial knowledge of the first or second grade. I never said "no" to myself.
To face a first month, by listening to the instructor without understanding	To study at least eight hours per day, listening to songs, attending movies in English, and	In one semester I passed from the sixth to the tenth grade, according to evaluations from instructors.

what was lectured about.	taking notes for five months/year. I self-assigned extra vocabulary homework, even by writing small essays.	The worry of failing was never present in my brain or behavior. Conscientiously or unconscientiously, I rejected failure.
To finish junior high school and transfer from Havana Business Academy to a university in two years	To obtain successful results, not only in English but also in typing and shorthand without being absent one single day from classes.	Finished junior and high school with flying colors. Being ready to start working as a bilingual English-Spanish secretary at sixteen years old, I was ready to work hard every single day.
With a monthly salary of $110, I saved $500 in a year self-financing my one-month trip to the US at seventeen years of age	To save money under financial austerity and small contributions to my family finances. I never thought of the word "failure" and rejected the idea of not being understood in English.	Successful three years as a bilingual stenographer plus studying the first two years of high school with outstanding grades. I was always ready to fulfill all assigned tasks and never felt afraid to ask my co-workers. For me, procrastination would have been to be afraid of making mistakes. When I failed, I recognized my fault as soon as I was aware of it.

My mother's manifestation of tenacity and overcoming procrastination were the following: a) starting and finishing secondary education with high grades after studying hard; b) persistent attendance; and c) passing all exams. When she was sixty years old, she could finish secondary education. She was the eldest student in the school groups. She was convinced that she was making a big effort to accomplish her goals and was never afraid of recognizing her mistakes. Her systematic effort and commitment to do her best created a sense of certainty and responsibility in her performance as a student. My father didn't allow her to work, although she was always ready to accept paid or unpaid work.

She could successfully simultaneously handle keeping the house satisfactorily clean and organized, participating in school extracurriculars, and in political activities. She was a leader of the Association of Cuban Women for some decades.

She exercised every morning at home for decades. She was very energetic, ready to undertake whatever task was assigned to, or by her. She never was late to any activity.

While my five-year bachelor's in economics, my one-year Master of Science in operational research in Scotland, and my doctorates, I always felt my mother's support either in person or mentally.

To cite an interesting situation related to my mother's tenacious influence on my extensive educational and scientific career, during my second PhD in the former Soviet Union. My last stay in Kyiv took place from April to September 1990. One month before the defense, my supervisor delivered the dissertation with plenty of mistakes to be corrected in a week in its three hundred pages. In mid-

August 1990 I left my supervisor's office holding my dissertation which needed to be partially retyped. I felt defeated. After eight years of systematic research, there was only one month to materialize my second Ph.D. I felt overwhelmed and returned to my dorm without imagining how would I redo the dissertation in three weeks. I was thinking about my mother asking me to solve the problem working hard without accepting defeat as of the following morning. I also meditated about my wife and my peers in Cuba. I had to do something.

Some hours later in the early morning I woke up, jumped from my bed, and said to myself: "Antonio, go ahead right now, and prepare yourself to do all the necessary corrections." Since I knew how to type in a Russian typing machine, I went to the Institute of Economics of the Ukrainian Academy of Sciences and asked for permission to start typing my dissertation. I could advance twenty pages at the end of the day. In a whole week, I could arrive only to page eighty. Procrastination made me feel pessimistic about my huge task. I was ready to do whatever I could because after eight years of overcoming obstacles, I had grown as a scientist in the Cuban sugar industry. On top of that, I felt my mother's presence asking me not to give up.

A pleasant surprise was waiting for me at the aforementioned library the Monday of the second week. As soon as I sat down to start typing, a smiling Ukrainian lady approached me letting me know that – since she had seen me working so hard, after talking to her boss and having his approval – she volunteered to type the dissertation herself without any financial compensation.

I could hardly believe my eyes or my ears. I felt as if God had sent me the lady as compensation for so much effort for eight years. Kissing her hand, I thanked her the best I could.

That day I called my mother and let her know that her youngest son would be ready to return to Cuba with his second Ph.D. at the end of September 1990.

As a happy ending to this special difficulty, which took me eight years to overcome, I always believed in myself, stood up whenever I fell, and defeated procrastination on several occasions. Thanks to my tenacity, inherited from my mother, I could become one of three Cuban economists holding two Ph.D.

Previously in this chapter, I mentioned the interesting topic of embracing optimism.

What does it mean to embrace optimism?

Being optimistic involves **believing that your future and your specific goals are possible**. Let your visions inspire you and pull you into the future. Practice visualizing a future where you achieve your goals, and where you see good things happening in the world.

Optimistic people have a positive outlook on the future and an inclination to view themselves as being in control of positive events. Optimism increases creativity and productivity. People who have hope for the future can focus on accomplishing tasks because they believe that their creative ideas will work.

Definition of optimism according to Google

Optimism and pessimism are mindsets—**ways of thinking and seeing things**. Optimists see the positive side of things. They expect things to turn out well. They believe they have the skill and ability to make good things happen.

An example of optimism is **believing that there will always be opportunities to make things better tomorrow, even if you are experiencing challenges today.**

Types of Optimism according to Google

Unrealistic optimism is when positive expectations and the actual evidence don't match. Comparative optimism is expecting good things for yourself as compared to another person. Situational optimism is the expectation of a good outcome in a specific situation.

My optimism has been comparative all the time because I expected to conquer very difficult goals based on my tenacity and brain capacity. Some of the challenges were presented to me with the option of accepting them; others were created by me.

One common attitude towards achieving high goals was never to give up, and never to say no to myself, whereas my behavior relates to my honest and straightforward actions orally or through body language. I always finished all the tasks (both assigned to me by superiors or by myself) not necessarily being always successful. I was always ready to admit my mistakes, as well as to rectify them as soon as possible.

Optimism and happiness in the context of physical exercising

Definition of Happiness

What is the best definition of happiness?

Happiness is **a sense of well-being, joy, or contentment**. When people are successful, safe, or lucky, they feel happiness.

https://www.vocabulary.com > dictionary > happiness

'Happiness is difficult to define because it means something different to each individual person. Nobody can fully understand or experience another person's feelings, and we all have our own particular passions from which we take pleasure.'

In her 2007 book The How of Happiness, positive psychology researcher **Sonja Lyubomirsky** elaborates, describing happiness as "the experience of joy, contentment, or positive well-being, combined with a sense that one's life is good, meaningful, and worthwhile."

My own definition of happiness. Along my eighty-two years of age, I have gone through different degrees of happiness in the context of opposite political systems, diverse economic situations, being a son, a father, a grandfather, a student, a professor, an advisor, a scholar, going through completely different marriages, being free, captive, religious, atheist, hopeful, desperate, sad due to losing somebody close to my heart, healthy, temporarily sick, desperate, encouraging, and fighting for a better future.

A type of happiness that characterizes my personality is to achieve important goals in my life, especially: 1) learning four foreign languages and using them with the confidence of understanding and being understood; 2) being grateful to the Lord because I had two important women in my life: a) my tenacious, active and loving mother: and b) my extraordinary second wife for forty years, six months and one day, in which she transformed me into a much better man going from being an egoist lady's man to becoming a loyal and empathetic husband. She taught me what real love meant in actions, feelings, and supporting each other, especially under enormously difficult circumstances; she was my rock, and I was hers. Not for a single moment during our long-lasting togetherness I had the slightest doubt of her love for me.; c) accomplishing all my main targets as student, scholar, professor, writer, inspirational speaker, singer in public, and especially human being; d) my legacy is to continue teaching through my books, even after my death; e) defeating or overcoming procrastination in the most transcendental intellectual battles of my life, especially learning English in two years in Cuba, becoming an instructor of my peers during my first college degree, my intense learning how to read, speak and write dissertations in Spanish and Russian, achieving my first doctorate in straight forward opposition of my Cuban peer scholars, presenting four pre-defenses and one successful final dissertation at the Institute of Economics of the Ukrainian Academy of Sciences, approving my second doctorate in Economics at the University of Havana, which was defended in Kiev a couple of months before the collapse of the Soviet Union; f) in confrontation with the Cuban dictator Fidel Castro I was able to create and to defend a scientific method of establishing the optimal crop period in the Sugar Industrial-Agricultural Complex of Cuba after twenty-five years research at the 155 sugar agriculture-industrial complexes, working for five years as advisor to the Cuban Minister of Sugar; g) after three years working as leader of a research team at the Merida Institute of Technology in Mexico, I could finally escape from Cuba arriving on Chicago in April 1996; h) from 1997 to 2016 I became faculty at DePaul University in Chicago, where I was recipient of the Excellence in Teaching Award in 2007. Finally, my wife and I achieved our American Dream in the first decade of the Twenty-first century.

I faced all challenges with the determination to overcome procrastination on the basis of tenacity. My happiness was long-lasting from 1954 in Cuba to 2006 in America deeply immersed in scientific endeavors. After 2006 my happiness materialized in becoming a prolific writer of ten non-fiction books in two publishers.

May God be praised for blessing and fostering my scientific career and my two feminine angels. I tried hard, but, whenever I felt to had restlessly fought without materializing the expected result, suddenly out of the blue the unlikely solution appeared.

In my so far eighty-two years old, I have been happy, with a smile on my face and eternal gratitude in my brain.

<u>Does the addition of being happy exercising contribute to obtaining good health?</u>

I recommend the readers to enter in YouTube and concentrate their attention on the story of Johanna Quass, a ninety-seven years old lady, who recommends the following exercises to keep healthy:

1. Sleep eight hours a day.
2. Have a plant-based diet, eat fruits and veggies, and neither overeats nor junk food. Drink a lot of water.
3. Active bed gymnastics every day, right after waking up, such as lifting the pelvis while stretching the legs, lifting, and lowering the shoulders, and pulling one elastic band behind your back.
4. Keep moving for at least one hour every day, briskly walking, dancing, etc.
5. To prevent mental aging and stimulate the brain, practice crosswords, and sudokus.
6. Be happy and enjoy life.
7. Exercise at home.

As a general concluding result, she states that "**Psyche's emotional state is more important than all the previous rules. To maintain the flexibility and elasticity of the muscles and the strength of the joints, stretching and strength exercises should be done daily.**"

As recently as March 3rd, 2023, out of the blue I discovered on YouTube the good news about Ms. Johanna Quass' positive experience of keeping healthy and optimistic at the advanced age of 97 years.

For the last three years, this author has been systematically exercising at home following instructions from three different physical therapists (PT) with the purpose of solving balance issues, avoiding falls, and incontinence. I was very fortunate to have been treated by them. There was something I discovered from my last treatment. I had the opportunity to meet several patients, some of whom had been treated by several PTs. Some of them had experienced one special issue for weeks, and after some months, the former issue came back again. Since I am a systematic exerciser, I asked them whether they had continued exercising after the treatment was over. My suspicion has been confirmed because most of them let me know that they had stopped exercising a few weeks after their treatments were over. The difference between them and me was that, as a result of being tenacious, I had been exercising for years after the treatments were over. In reality, whenever I exercise, I combine exercises to improve balance, I have not fallen, and my incontinence has been partially reduced. The difference between the consulted patients and me was that I am a tenacious person in most of the activities I carry out.

It was a surprise to compare my regular exercising practices with Johanna's and conclude that, as a matter of fact, inadvertently I had been following almost all her steps or actions taken to achieve the goal of becoming healthier. To illustrate the similarity of our ways to improve our health, I have built Table # 2.

Table No. 2:

Comparison between Ms. Quass, and this author's, healthy procedures

Johanna's customary activities	Antonio Morales-Pita's
1. Sleep eight hours/day	Since January 2023, 7 to 8 hours /day. Going to bed from 8:30 to 9:30 pm
2. Plant-based diet (fruits and veggies) never overeating or junk food. Drinking a lot of water	Fruit and veggies during breakfast, lunch, and dinner). Proteins (fish, chicken breast, and turkey). Never overeating or junk food. At least 6 glasses of water daily
3. Daily bed gymnastics	Totally in agreement, at least for 30 minutes/day
4. Keep moving for at least one hour every day, briskly walking, and dancing,	Totally in agreement, walking every day at least one mile in winter and four to five miles during the remaining seasons
5. Stimulate the brain by practicing crosswords, sudoku	Totally in agreement, adding variety in introducing changes in formerly customary physical procedures. Daily practice of sudoku since my arrival in the US, since 1996
6. Be happy enjoying life	Singing and rejecting pessimistic thoughts. Systematic defeating procrastination. Being predominantly tenacious and optimistic, always doing whatever is required to accomplish a goal
7. Exercise at home	Daily exercising at home for 0.5 to 1.5 hours (including stationary bike and elliptical equipment)

Food for thought:

1. What is the main reason why, after taking physical therapy training exercises, a large number of patients stop physical exercising?
2. After reading and meditating on the healthy procedures pointed out in Table No. 2, would some readers feel motivated to imitate Johanna's and Antonio's customary activities?
3. Out of the seven customary activities, have any readers found which is the most important one to keep being healthy?
4. From the readers' points of view, are there any of the seven customary activities hardest to be applied to their lives?

Chapter II
Percentage of Immigrant Seniors in the US Senior Population

"Old age is like everything else. To make a success of it, you've got to start young."
– Theodore Roosevelt.
"Wrinkles should merely indicate where smiles have been."
– Mark Twain.

This author found an interesting paper about elderly immigrants in the United States taken from https//www.prob.org > resources >elderly-immigrants.

The U.S. elderly immigrant population rose from 2.7 million in 1990 to 4.6 million in 2010, a *70 percent increase* in 20 years (see figure).

The U.S. Foreign-born population aged 65 + Increased Substantially Between 1990 and 2010

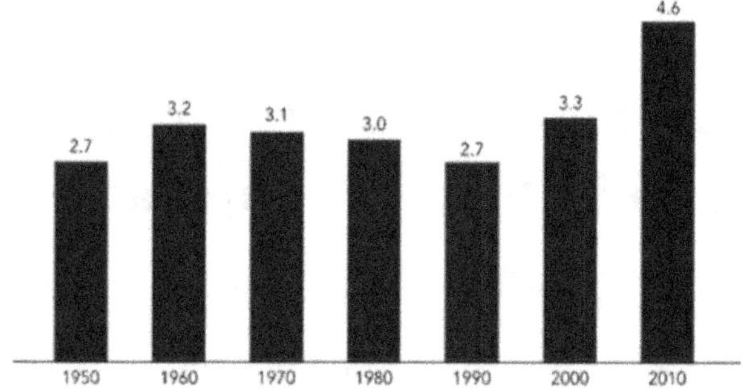

Source: U.S. Census Bureau, historical census data 1950-2000; and Current Population Survey, 2010.

Aging World and U.S. Population Trends

In 2010, more than one in eight U.S. adults ages 65 and older were foreign-born, a share that is expected to continue to grow. The U.S. elderly immigrant population rose from 2.7 million in 1990 to 4.6 million in 2010, a 70 percent increase in 20 years (see figure). This issue of *Today's Research on Aging* reviews recent research examining older immigrants in the United States, conducted by National Institute on Aging (NIA)-supported researchers and others. Understanding both the unique characteristics of elderly foreign-born adults and the challenges some of them face is important as policymakers and planners address the well-being and health of the United States' aging population.

The U.S. foreign-born population consists of individuals living in the United States who were not U.S.

citizens at birth. In 2020—the most recent data from the American Community Survey (ACS)—an estimated 44.1 million foreign-born people resided in the United States, representing 13.5% of the total U.S. population.

According to the Center for Immigration Studies {*https://cis.org*} the 47.9 million foreign-born residents (legal and illegal) in September 2022 is the largest number ever recorded by the US government.

Demographic Trends

Fueling the growth of the U.S. immigrant population ages 65 and older are two trends—the aging of the long-term foreign-born population and the recent migration of older adults as part of family reunification and refugee admissions. Analysis of American Community Survey data suggests that 10 percent of immigrants ages 65 and older had been in the country for fewer than 10 years in 2010. Most U.S. immigrants who settle in this country after age 60 are sponsored by their adult children who had immigrated to the United States as young adults.

Long-term immigrants who arrived in the United States as children or young adults tend to face challenges similar to their U.S.-born peers. By contrast, immigrants who migrate after age 60 are often a "potentially vulnerable population" due to limited English language proficiency, little or no U.S. work experience, and weak ties to social institutions, reports Judith Wilmoth of Syracuse University. They face rules barring them from participating in most entitlement and welfare programs unless they become naturalized citizens, but their language skills and age are often barriers to naturalization. Compared to immigrants who arrive earlier in life, late-life immigrants are more likely to be female, to have low education levels, to have limitations in physical functioning, and to be widowed.

Economic Circumstances

Foreign-born elderly tend to have less personal income than U.S.-born elderly, on average. Reliance on a different mix of economic resources in old age accounts for some of the income differences between immigrant and U.S.-born elderly, according to George Borjas of Harvard University. In 2007, U.S.-born elderly ages 65 and older were considerably more likely than immigrant elderly to receive Social Security benefits, investment income, and retirement benefits such as pensions. Immigrant elderlies were more likely to be employed than U.S.-born elderly, driven in part by incentives related to Social Security program eligibility.

Immigrant elderlies are more likely to have incomes below the poverty line than U.S.-born elderly. In 2010, 8 percent of U.S.-born elderly lived below the poverty threshold, compared to 16 percent of foreign-born elderly. The U.S. Census Bureau estimates that within the foreign-born population ages 65 and older, 15 percent of Asian immigrants, 21 percent of all Hispanic immigrants, and 23 percent of Mexican immigrants lived below the poverty line in 2010.

The publication also explores recent research on the living arrangements, life expectancy, health, and disability levels of older immigrants in the United States.

Going through the aforementioned paragraphs, this author has concluded that:

1. The U.S. foreign-born population has experienced a noticeable increase from 4.6 million in 2010 to 44.1 million in 2020 and 47.9 million in 2022.
2. The reasons for this explosion of foreign immigrants from the south border of Texas relate to the worsening economic and political situations of Latin American countries.
3. During the presidencies of Obama, Trump, and Biden, this increase of foreign immigrants has been one important issue resulting from the unparallel socio-politico-economic situations of Latin American countries with the United States.

Chapter III
Love Relationships in Senior Couples

Happiness in marriage is a moment of choice. A decision to love, forgive, grow, and grow old together.
– Faun Weaver

It doesn't matter how old people are. It matters if they love each other and have fun with each other.
– unknown

The love we have in our youth is superficial compared to the love an old man has for his old wife.
– Will Durant

What percentage of seniors are married?

According to a report[1]: **At least 9 in 10 adults ages 60 or older have been married**. Specifically, 91% of men and 92% of women ages 60 to 69 and 95% of both men and women ages 70 or older have been married. These estimates are much higher than for all men (63%) and women (69%)

---

[1]https://www.census.gov/library/publications/2021/demo/p70-167.html

ages 15 or older.

According to the paper Number, Timing, and Duration of Marriages and Divorces: 20161 Current Population Reports By Yerís Mayol-García, Benjamin Gurrentz, and Rose M. Kreider Issued April 2021:

1) By 2016, the median age at first marriage had risen approximately 2 full years since 2008, to 30 for men and 28 for women. •

2) Among ever-married adults 20 years and over, 34 percent of women and 33 percent of men had ever been divorced, while the percentage ever divorced was highest for adults aged 55 to 64 (about 43 percent for both sexes). •

3) Among race and Hispanic origin groups, ever-married Asian women and men had the lowest proportion ever divorced (14 percent and 11 percent respectively).

4) Women who divorced in the previous 12 months were more likely than recently divorced men to be in poverty (20 percent compared with 11 percent, respectively).

5) Among ever-married adults 20 years and over, 14 percent of women had ever been widowed.

6) Love and Loss Among Older Adults nine in ten adults ages 70 or older have married, but over half of women, and a quarter of men ages 75 or older, who have been married, have experienced widowhood.

7) At least 9 in 10 adults ages 60 or older have been married. Specifically, 91% of men and 92% of

women ages 60 to 69 and 95% of both men and women ages 70 or older have been married. These estimates are much higher than for all men (63%) and women (69%) ages 15 or older.

These estimates are much higher than for all men (63%) and women (69%) ages 15 or older.

Many older adults remained in their marriage for a long period of time. Among adults who married in the 1970s, at least half reached their 25th anniversary.

At least 59% of adults ages 60 or older have been married just once. Among those ages 60 to 69 years, 46% of men and 39% of women are still married to the first and only person they wed.

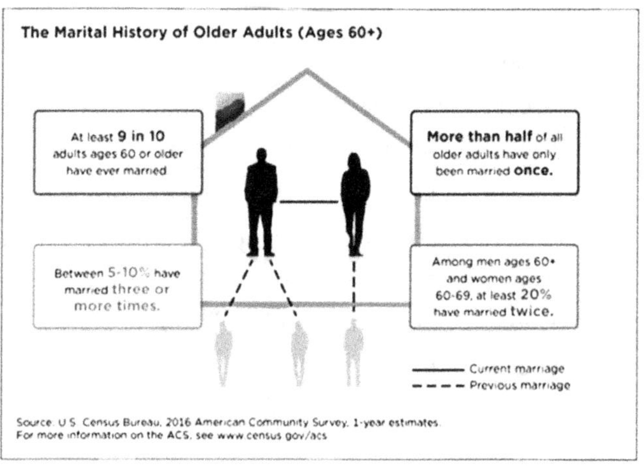

Divorce

With marriage comes the risk of marital dissolution via divorce or widowhood, which have both been prevalent among older adults.

While 34% of women and 33% of men ages 20 or older who ever married had ever divorced, the percentage of adults 55 to 64 years who divorced is much higher: about 43% for both sexes.

Although significantly lower when compared with 55- to 64-year-olds, high rates of divorce persist for those 65 to 74 years at 39%, which is still higher than for the general adult population. For adults aged 75 or older, the rate is lower at 24%.

Since the 1990s, the national trend of divorce among adults 50 years or older has risen, often linked to the marital instability of the aging baby boomer generation.

Widowhood

Divorce is not the only marital disruption that older adults face. They also disproportionately represent a large percentage of those who become widows or widowers in a given year.

Among adults 15 or older widowed in the preceding 12 months, 71% of men and 69% of women were 65 or older, even though this age group comprises only 19% of all people ages 15 or older.

Widowhood is particularly common among older women compared to older men due to differences in life expectancies. Women on average live longer than men.

Among those 75 years or older who had ever married, 58% of women and 28% of men had experienced the death of a spouse in their lifetime, making this stage of life particularly difficult for older adults.

The proportion of those who are currently widowed is relatively lower than for those widowed at one point because some respondents who lost a spouse eventually remarried, becoming "currently married" instead of "currently widowed."

Nonetheless, differences between the sexes persist among those 75 years or older: 54% of women and 20% of men were currently widowed at the time of the interview.

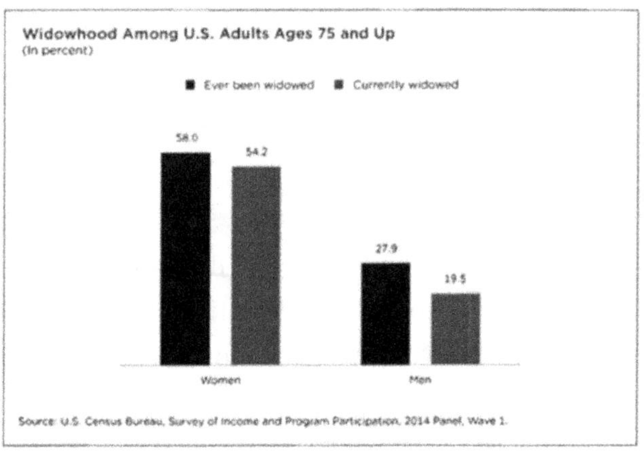

Remarriage

After divorce and widowhood, many older adults say "I do" again at some point in their life.

Among men and women 60 to 69 years old, 23% had married twice and less than 10% had married three times or more. Among those ages 70 or older, 22% of men and 19% of women had married twice while 8% of men and 6% of women had married three times or more.

In other words, older adults have a rich marital history that reflects the diverse experiences of long commitment, loss via divorce or widowhood, and new partnerships as they age.

The above data were provided by *Benjamin Gurrentz, who is a survey statistician in the Census Bureau's Survey Improvement Research Branch, and Yeris Mayol-Garcia, who is a statistician demographer in the Fertility and Family Statistics Branch.*

Food for thought:

1. Have any senior readers, who might be in the process of getting married or divorced, feel identified with any of the two representations, Marital History of Older Adults, and Widowhood among Adults?
2. Analyzing the second graph about the transit from ever being widowhood to currently being a widow shows a small difference of only 3.9 for women and almost 9% for men. Which reasons might be the cause of this difference?

Chapter IV
To Be in Control of Your Health

"There is no normal life that is free of pain. It's the very wrestling with our problems that can be the impetus for our growth."
– Fred Rogers

"Our wounds are often the openings into the best and most beautiful part of us."
– David Richo

"Just because no one else can heal or do your inner work for you doesn't mean you can, should, or need to do it alone."
– Lisa Olivera

Is It Possible for seniors to be in control of their health?

This author's answer is yes as long as the following premises are valid: 1) The senior should have some elementary physical training – for example, walking some miles as well as elementary exercises on a daily basis; 2) receives physical training; 3) has a basic control about elementary parameters of his health like measuring his blood pressure, has once or twice doctors' appointment in a year; 4) pays attention to unhealthy signals from his body, such as frequent headaches, swelling in the legs or in any other part of his body, experiences fever, sleeping less than six or seven hours per day, and so on.

My behavior in relation to the premises listed in the preceding paragraph is the following: 1. I exercise every day as follows: thirty minutes of balance on a mattress, walking from four miles in spring, summer, and fall to two miles in winter; every other day thirty minutes of balance plus sixty minutes in elliptical and bike plus walking; 2. I have received three physical trainings for improving balance, reducing incontinence, and avoiding falls; 3. measuring my blood pressure every day, punctual attendance to all my doctors' appointments and strictly following their instructions; 4. whenever I discover swellings or unrecognized pains in whatever part of my body, rushing to immediate care, doctor's offices or even emergency rooms.

Is It Possible for seniors to physically and mentally be prepared to physical exercising?

My answer is "yes". Some days I might feel "not willing to exercise" for whatever reason; but, nonetheless, I force myself to take action without any exception, and almost immediately starting my body feels comfortable and satisfied using my tenacity without allowing procrastination signals presence in my brain. My commitment to defeat procrastination is always present in my mind. Readers are highly recommended to read my book *Grit + Tenacity + Proactiveness Pulling the Bull by the Horns.* This is a detailed narration of defeating postponing actions throughout my entire life.

To feel in control of one's health is a good way to say to one's brain "Never say 'no' to yourself". Do not allow negative thoughts to appear in your way toward positive actions benefiting your health.

Although this author has always immediately "stood up after a fall", this doesn't mean that unexpected inconveniences have never appeared in his life. After some hours of inaction, like when I was about to conclude the final version of my second dissertation in Kyiv, Ukraine, the following morning I woke up ready to do whatever it took. I had immense work to do, but I decided to cross out all the mistaken pieces in about three or four hours and to type a new document in Russian. I had previously learned how to type in a Russian machine and went to the library of the Institute of Economics of the Ukrainian Academy of Sciences, and asked for permission to use their Russian machines. I had to type three hundred pages. For one week I could only advance 45 pages, and there were only two weeks before the defense of the dissertation. In the second week, I was ready to continue redoing the dissertation, but suddenly the secretary of the library approached me and offered to retype the remaining pages without asking for any remuneration. The Lord made the miracle happen. In conclusion, I had no choice but to defend the dissertation on the originally scheduled date. Procrastination was defeated once again.

Does procrastination appear in seniors if they decide to exercise?

The former paragraph positively answers this question because this writer was fifty years old when the aforementioned huge inconvenience appeared in my life. The passing of time doesn't preclude the appearance of procrastination in seniors. The longer a person lives, the more occasions he/she will have to meet obstacles in their lives. The decision to exercise, especially if it is due to solving health issues, will allow human beings to persevere in their attempts to benefit their health by enjoying life.

For seniors who are not used to exercising, it is possible to incorporate exercise into their lives.

In my opinion, the happier a person lives, the higher should be his/her chances to incorporate physical exercise as long as his/her health is acceptable, or even better, in good shape.

Before having a heart attack when I was fifty-eight years old, I was not a systematic exerciser. My life was full of content and, suddenly, I started to fear death. So, I decided to live following advice from doctors, nurses, and physical therapists. My inborn tenacity made me pay full attention and change my habit towards increasing exercise systematically, eating healthily, and not allowing any exceptions to take place. Shortly afterwards, I could witness slowly reducing weight, discarding fatty foods, feeling my muscles stronger, and so on.

Is it possible for seniors to persuade themselves that it is almost never too late to be in control of their health?

There are seniors with a whole range of mental attitudes, such as optimistic, pessimistic, brave, and ready to fight procrastination, indifferent to trying new perspectives, hopeful to find cures to their sicknesses, being in true love with their partners, living surrounded by a lovely family, healthy, and unwholly.

The healthier they are, it looks reasonable to expect their likely acceptance to be in control of their health. There are seniors who have normally taken good care of their health in their younger years, who would most likely change unhealthy habits for better ones.

As a conclusion, it is very difficult to generalize the senior's concerns about persuading them to be in control of their health. Seniors enjoying happy married lives for decades will be the most likely candidates to pay attention to their lives. To be in love is a solid reason to enjoy life and share it with their partners. According to the Merriam-Webster dictionary, a partner is defined as "one associated with another, especially in an action; a person with whom one shares an intimate relationship: one member of a couple".

When I was a fourteen-year-old young man, one of my favorite "teachers" in the process of learning English as a second language was Nat King Cole, one of whose songs was "Love is a many-splendored thing". I am a fortunate human being to love and be loved by two special women: my mother, and my second wife, Gladys, to whom I dedicated my book Gladys, *May Unforgettable Love.*

In this author's prolonged eighty-three years age, living in all European, north, central, and South American countries, Australia, New Zealand, Singapore, Dubai, Morocco, Egypt, Israel, Greece, India, and Jordan as a tourist, scholar, and prolific writer, he has found out that love is a reason to be living; and, consequently, quite likely to be in control of one's health.

My prolific life as a traveler of the world is narrated in my book *Is It Always Fun to Travel Abroad?* which contains sound advice for traveling around the world, which contains the following two paragraphs:

There are two extremes that I recommend the readers <u>avoid</u>:

a) <u>Firstly, do not travel to the point that you go into debt and have to pay the cost of traveling for several years.</u> It is always necessary to save as much as we can without sacrificing the enjoyment of life. For example, I wanted to go to Italy when I was eighteen years old in Cuba (in my country, especially after the revolution, that became impossible). When I was in my early fifties I was working in Mexico. I was obliged to contribute 70% of my income to the Cuban government and saw the opportunity of traveling abroad, but that was impossible for financial and political reasons. In my late fifties, I arrived in the US and became a free man, so there were no political difficulties, but I needed to build my life in this great country, so I had to work very hard, to build my credit and buy a home. When I turned 66, I had paid more than 50% of my mortgage, I had no debts, and I had savings that allowed my wife and I to spend five or six thousand dollars on travel. We preferred to buy a home close to our workplace living in Chicago – whose public transportation is acceptable – and decided not to buy a car. So, when I turned sixty-six years old, my wife and I went to Italy, that is to say, forty-eight years after dreaming about visiting Italy. Now, when we went to Italy, we had totally paid for the trip in advance, we only had to spend money, using our credit card, for petty expenditures, such as food, taxis, and so on. Of course, we paid our credit cards in full. I do not pretend, or even suggest, to the readers to wait decades to materialize their traveling dreams, but I do wish to recommend them to make sure that their credit ratings are not negatively affected, and that they can pay their monthly credit card bills in full. It is so wonderful to know that one does not pay a single cent in interest and that one can pay his/her mortgage promptly and with some extra money to reduce the principal. It is very important that one pays all bills in full and on time.

b) <u>Secondly, do not die with huge amounts of money in the bank without having enjoyed traveling</u>. I know so many cases in this country of hard-working people who were able to accumulate huge amounts of money for their old ages, but then they did not exercise, take care of their health, pay attention to their basic ways of enjoying life, and their money was used by other people who did not work to make it. Being a Christian I firmly believe that the Lord gave us options. He wished us to be happy and kind to humanity, to be empathetic, but also to take care of ourselves. If He gave us some talents, let's use them, and be happy.

Relationship between exercising, healthy eating, and positive mental attitude

The formerly cited three factors are not necessarily related, but there is no argument against the fact that, whenever they simultaneously exist in any normal individual, the possessor of the three should definitely have chances of living longer, and much happier than those who do not possess them at the same time.

Searching for definitions of "happiness" In her 2007 book *The How of Happiness,* positive psychology researcher Sonja Lyubomirsky elaborates, describing happiness as "the experience of joy, contentment, or positive well-being, combined with a sense that one's life is good, meaningful, and worthwhile." Taken from *https://greatergood.berkeley.edu › topic › definition.*

What is my opinion about the three words and happiness? Analyzing each of the components, I can ascertain that without physical exercise it is impossible to have good health, especially the longer the individual lives.

The readers are recommended to consult the following link recommended by the National Institute on Aging: *"https://www.nia.nih.gov/health/topics/exercise-and-physical-activity"*

Tips to Boost Your Health as You Age:

1. Exercise and Physical Activity Tracking Tools. Keeping track of your progress is a great way to stay motivated to exercise. Use these tracking tools to help stick to your exercise routine.

2. What four types of exercise should you do as you grow older? Try endurance, flexibility, strength, and balance activities to stay independent for longer.

3. No matter your health and physical abilities, you can gain a lot by staying active. Learn about the many benefits of being physically active.

4. Tips for older adults to stay motivated to exercise. Try to make exercise a priority. Remember that being active is one of the most important things you can do each day to maintain and improve health. Try these tips to help you stay motivated to exercise.

5. Some people like to walk on a treadmill at the gym. Others find that kind of activity boring. The key to sticking with exercise is to <u>make it interesting and enjoyable</u>. Be creative. Do things you enjoy but pick up the pace. Do all <u>four types of exercise</u>—endurance, strength, balance, and flexibility. The variety helps keep things interesting! Try some new activities to keep your interest alive.

6. Find ways to fit exercise into your day. Look for easy ways to add physical activity to your regular schedule:
   - Take the stairs instead of the elevator.

- Take a walk with co-workers during your lunch break. An exercise buddy can help you stick with your plan to be more active!
- Walk down the hall and talk with a co-worker instead of sending an e-mail.
- Park a little farther away from your office and enjoy the walk.
- Join your company's fitness center if there is one.

7. Keep track of your exercise progress. The best way to stay motivated is to measure and celebrate your successes: a) Make an exercise and physical activity plan that works for you and track your daily physical activity; b) Find new ways to increase your physical activity; c) Keep track of your monthly progress to see improvement, and d) Update your exercise plan as you progress.

Analysis of the Morales-Pita's family approach to physical exercising

Siria Pita Allende. My mother was my first example of approaching and introducing physical exercise in my life. From an early age, I saw my mother exercising at home, running from the front door through a long hall to the backyard of the home. She never stopped doing so through decades. She was always thin, never overate, and kept very active the whole day. I had three siblings, who never followed my mother's example. I did exercise by participating in physical activities in the school and in classes about walking and running in the stadium of the school. For my mother, there were no vacations for exercising, and I tried to imitate her. My brother did exercise volleyball and baseball, although I never saw him running. He married at nineteen years old, and then he started to work without any physical exercise. Neither of my two sisters ever exercised. My mother died at 88 years old when she overdosed at a Christmas party and suffered a stroke.

Florentino Morales. My father was a very strong man whose childhood took place in the countryside of Havana. His first job at eight years old was to tame horses and maintain his mother and three sisters. He worked as a stevedore for forty years in Havana's main food market. He was so healthy that I never remember ever seeing or hearing of my father's being sick, not even a standard cold. He exercised daily as part of his job. He only visited a doctor when he was in his seventies and had to be operated on for cancer in his prostate. He was never hospitalized and did not know that he had cancer. My father died when he overestimated his strength holding twelve cubes full of soil from the backyard to the garden of the house. He died of a stroke in less than two days. He also died at 88, twenty years before my mother.

I arrived in the United States escaping from communism at age fifty-six. Before coming to the US, I was working in Mexico leading a research team, and – as far as I can remember – I was not a systematic exerciser before arriving in this country. Although I loved to run during my stay in Cuba, I didn't do it in a systematic way.

In my first two years in the US, I was teaching at DePaul University and two other colleges, besides working as a translator English-Spanish, and was able to translate one book from English to Spanish. Suddenly in my third year, I experienced some sort of painful discomfort around my chest or upper stomach, for some weeks. I thought that my discomfort was due to stress, but my wife sensed that something was going wrong with my health. After a week, she forced me to go to a hospital and pushed me inside a taxi. As soon as I arrived at the hospital, I excused myself because I thought that my health was all right. One minute after being examined by a doctor, he let me know that I was having a heart attack. My weight was 194 pounds.

From pages 43 and 44 of my book *Gladys, My Unforgettable Love*, I copied those tense moments:

Then I was really afraid and was immediately taken to the hospital area for heart problems. My wife was crying incessantly and called our spiritual father because we thought that I needed the extreme unction. Reverend Morales arrived immediately and found Gladys crying desperately, asking the Lord to take her instead of me.

At the hospital, she was beside me and asked the nurses which were the symptoms or the numbers in the boards that would elicit immediate action. At the first sign of urgency, she ran for the nurse, took her to the room, and showed her the numbers. The danger was immediate. The cardiologist would be there in less than half an hour.

While I was being transferred on the stretcher to the operating room, Gladys was crying desperately. Silently and with a smile on my face, I prayed and thanked the Lord for His blessings—my exceptional wife, incredible mother, scholarly career, students in Cuba, Mexico, and the United States, books, and children—and commended myself to Him. When waking up from the anesthesia, I could only see a mist. I was surprised to be alive.

Here is an incredible example of Gladys' commitment to me. She was seated by my side in the room. My wife received instructions not to let me touch the wound in my groin until it was healed. Being unconscious, there was a risk that I might involuntarily touch it. I had been given an angioplasty with a stent in the central artery of my heart. Gladys was beside me all the time without sleeping or eating for four days, taking care of my groin, and looking at the numbers on the board. After that time, the cardiologist told her of my survival of the heart attack. Then she fainted. The doctor told me that she was stressed without any heart problems. I did not know how to compensate her for so much love, so much care, and so much dedication. When I asked her, she only said with a smile on her face and watery eyes: "The best reward I can have is that you are alive."

After realizing that I had been so close to death, I was done to do whatever it took me to avoid a second heart attack.

After recovering from the heart attack, I was subject to several sessions of exercising, and most importantly important talks and films about ways of healthy eating, and the consequences of not exercising.

My life changed for the better in the following ways: a) I reduced my weight from 194 lbs. to 160 from 1998 to 2010; and to 140 from 2010 to 2020; since 2021 my weight has gone down to 135. I never went back beyond the previously mentioned weight; b) I started to exercise systematically every day without missing one day; c) I was treated by three physical therapists for improving balance, reducing incontinence, and avoiding falls; and finally, d) since 2020 I have started to walk at least two miles per day.

Food for thought:

1. The readers are suggested to meditate if they are physically and mentally prepared to start exercising.
2. Is it possible for them to start exercising with a qualified PT, and continue doing so after the sessions are over?
3. Are they ready to overcome procrastination when pessimistic feelings affect their decisions to keep exercising after the PT sessions are over?

Chapter V
Interrelationship Between Systematic Exercising, Self-Assurance, and Joy

"I sometimes wonder whether all pleasures are not substituted for joy."
– C. S. Lewis

"The most profound joy has more gravity than gaiety in it."
– Michel de Montaigne

"People are just as happy as they make up their minds to be."
– Abraham Lincoln

"Learn to let go. That is the key to happiness."
– Buddha

"The joy in life is to be used for a purpose. I want to be used when I die."
– George Bernard Shaw

"Whenever I need to do or to acquire something, I never say no to myself."
– Antonio E. Morales-Pita

What is systemic exercise?

Exercise also leads to what is called a systemic effect, which is the impact that the entire exercise session has on the whole body in terms of stimulus.

<u>What is systematic exercise?</u>

Exercise also leads to what is called a systemic effect, which is the impact that the entire exercise session has on the whole body in terms of stimulus.

The introduction of self-assurance, happiness, and joy in the context of improving memory

Definitions of self-assurance, happiness, and joy.
Self-assurance

Confidence in one's own abilities or character.

<u>Deep meaning of self-assurance:</u>

It means that the individual accepts and trusts him or herself and has a sense of control in life. That human being deeply knows his/her strengths and weaknesses and has a positive view of his/herself, by means of setting realistic expectations and goals, easily communicating assertively, and being able to handle criticism.

Someone who has self-assurance shows confidence in the things he/she says and does since the individual is sure of his/her abilities.

Synonyms of self-assurance are confidence, self-confidence, poise, and nerve to undertake and to make certain decisions, such as to begin, to commerce, to initiate, to launch, and to shoulder a new project. Is there any possibility that procrastination might appear in his/her way to block his intentions? Well, it may appear, but – in this author's opinion – his/her assurance should help in overcoming it.

Is there a relationship between self-assurance and happiness and joy?

Happiness

Is it possible to introduce happiness into systematic physical exercises? Physical exercises might be somewhat tedious if they are deprived of some sort of mental need and requirement. According to Google, "In a business context, needs and requirements are two separate entities, and converting business needs into specific measurable, relevant requirements is very important for the success of a business".

Would human beings, especially if they are seniors, be ready to incorporate happiness in their exercises as a need? This author's opinion and personal experience introducing happiness in his systematic daily exercises depend upon how tenacious the senior is.

As I have mentioned in several of my books, one of the most important reasons why physical therapist patients stop exercising some days after the end of their treatments is their lack of tenacity. In other words, once they feel better, they stop exercising because they are not tenacious. Generally speaking, in this author's opinion, procrastination commences to appear in their awareness (for example through postponements, reducing the number of exercise days or the time of the sessions, or even inventing reasons).

This author exercises every day, despite the fact that on some occasions, he has to force himself to start the session. How does he manage to impose his will to momentary idleness, inactivity, inaction, or inertia? By adding awareness of improvements in the quality and extension of the exercises, inventing new ones, adding encouraging songs, and starting to recognize or even discover improvements in his muscles.

This author has found an interesting article about tenacity in Nancy Solari:

https://www.lifehack.org/911625/what-is-tenacity

Tenacity

Tenacity is what makes you leap out of bed each day. You might not have discovered what this spark is yet, but it is somewhere within you. Becoming a more determined person and utilizing this quality can allow you to be more successful. Here are four ways to use tenacity that will yield measurable results.

1) Put in preparation (In all aspects of life, the tenacious person takes the time to prepare for the future. This makes achieving your goals easier and you will find that you are more efficient).

2) Be forward-looking. To be a more determined person, you need to live in the present moment. Exert your energy in focusing on what is to come. Think about where you might see yourself living in the future.

3) Seek opportunities. If you show that you are open to <u>new opportunities</u>, you will have more chances to succeed.

4) Know your worth. <u>Understanding your worth</u> and how others view you helps you live with more tenacity.

Are the words happiness and joy synonyms?

Joy endures hardship and trials and connects with meaning and purpose. A person pursues happiness but chooses joy.

Happiness is an outward expression. Happiness comes from external factors such as material things, people, places, and experiences.

Joy is a more internal feeling that comes from being at peace with who you are and what you have achieved.

Happiness is more linked to external factors so, when something goes wrong, your happiness is also affected primarily. Having joy feels more secure and stable.

Happiness includes good feelings that relationships, friends, traveling, and memories give you, while joy is something you have despite things not going your way. Despite being uncertain, you feel security and peace with what you do. Joy lasts much longer than happiness ever will.

Differences between joy and happiness

Joy comes from within you, so it is not affected by negative external circumstances. When you have joy, you find it easier to be happy; but you find it much more difficult to be happier without joy. Joy comes from within you and doesn't fluctuate according to external aspects.

You are more fulfilled when you strive for joy than from happiness.

Happiness depends on others and mostly stems from your inability to be alone and stand on your own.

Joy comes from within, morality, is self-sufficient, and lasts longer.

Joy is long-lasting and doesn't rely on external sources. Joy comes from within you and doesn't fluctuate according to external impacts. Joy is a state of mind. Happiness is an emotion while joy is a state of mind.

Tips to improve memory

Since I turned eighty years old, I have been observing lapses of lack of memory. I normally get upset because I insist on remembering given words or expressions, but the more I try to force my mind, the more oblivious I become. I have gone through three types of psychological tests every two years, about the situation of my retention capacity, and the results appear to be somewhat similar. Therefore, I have concluded that, at the very least, no sign of Alzheimer's has so far been discovered. I am an active and prolific writer. From 2016 to mid-2023, I have published six books, and by the end of 2023, I should have published a total of eleven books. Since I was a professor for fifty-four years publishing six scholarly books plus two non-fiction ones, at the end of 2023, I should have published six + two + eleven books, nineteen books.

Given the fact that I taught for fifty-four years in Cuba, Mexico, and the United States, and continue teaching through my books, my legacy is precisely to continue teaching after my death.

Tips to improve the readers' memory. I have built a special table containing seven tips taken from the Mayo Clinic Staff to which I have added my personal experience.

Memory loss: 7 tips to improve your memory. Try these simple ways to improve your memory. By Mayo Clinic Staff	Dr. Antonio E. Morales-Pita's recommendation to improve memory through exercising in comparison with Mayo's tips to improve memory.
1. Be physically active every day Physical activity raises blood flow to the whole body, including the brain. This might help keep your memory sharp. For most healthy adults, the Department of Health and Human Services recommends a) at least 150 minutes a week of moderate aerobic activity, such as brisk walking, or b)75 minutes a week of vigorous aerobic activity, such as jogging. It's best if this activity is spread throughout the week. If you don't have time for a full workout, try a few 10-minute walks throughout the day.	I exercise through three types of activities: a) I walk every day between 2 and 3 miles, in which I spend an average of 60 minutes per day. b) Exercises for balance and incontinence on a mattress every day for 45 minutes. c) Every other day strong exercises for strengthening muscles in arms, and legs investing 60 minutes. d) In a normal week, I exercise as follows: 1. 60 minutes 7 days per week, for a total of 420 minutes of walking. 2. Exercises on the mattress: 45 x 7 = 315 minutes. 3. Vigorous activity 60 minutes x 3.5 = 210 minutes

	4. In total $420 + 315 + 210 = 945$ minutes per week.
2. Stay mentally active Just as physical activity keeps your body in shape, activities that engage your mind help keep your brain in shape. And those activities might help prevent some memory loss. Do crossword puzzles. Read. Play games. Learn to play a musical instrument. Try a new hobby. Volunteer at a local school or with a community group	Physical activity engages my mind and keeps my brain in shape. 1. Writing manuscripts for staying mentally active. Seven days per week with a minimum of 5 hours/day = 35 hours. 2. Singing 3.5 days per week for one hour totaling 3.5 hours. 3. Doing sudoku puzzles three days per week for forty-five minutes. 4. Selling my books thrice per week for three hours, totaling nine hours per week. 5. A total of 124 minutes per week.
3. Spend time with others Social interaction helps ward off depression and stress. Both of those can contribute to memory loss. Look for opportunities to get together with loved ones, friends, and other people, especially if you live alone.	One hour per week, totaling 60 minutes I keep busy all the time. I am never lazy and carefully plan all my activities. I have very few friends, normally seeing each other at least once per month.
4. Stay organized You're more likely to forget things if your home is cluttered or your notes are in disarray. Keep to-do lists up to date. Check off items you've finished. Keep your other essential items in a set place in your home.	I spend 30 minutes per day organizing my work and taking notes on my agenda. Thanks to my wife, who died 7.5 years ago, she constantly insisted on organizing my papers regarding manuscripts, making lists every day, and emphasizing that – whenever

Don't do too many things at once. If you focus on the information that you're trying to remember, you're more likely to recall it later. It also might help to connect what you're trying to remember to a favorite song or a familiar saying or idea	I enter my home, I place my keys, wallet, iPhone, and traveling ID in their fixed places. To misplace an item may happen but much less as it happened while my wife was alive.
5. Sleep well Not getting enough sleep has been linked to memory loss. Adults should sleep 7 to 9 hours a night on a regular basis.	After being treated by several specialists in controlling my sleeping hours, my average of sleeping ranges from 6.5 to 8 hours per day
6. Eat a healthy diet A healthy diet is good for your brain. Eat fruit, vegetables, and whole grains. Choose low-fat protein sources, such as fish, beans, and skinless poultry. What you drink also counts. Too much alcohol can lead to confusion and memory loss.	I have never smoked, or drunk alcohol, not even coffee. I have a very healthy diet consisting of: Breakfast: 100% fresh fruits, no juice, with a minimum of salt; lunch: one protein (chicken without scan and fat; turkey (7% fat); fish (no shellfish, shrimp), no ham or processed meats, rice and beans; and finally, dinner very similar to lunch without adding sweets like chocolate, cakes, and so on.
7. Manage chronic health problems Follow your healthcare provider's advice for dealing with medical conditions. The better you take care of yourself, the better your memory is likely to be. Regularly review the medicines you take with your health care provider.	I take good care of my health by keeping in close contact with all the doctors. I always rush to the doctor whenever I detect some irregularity, pain, or swelling in any part of my body. My hospital is Northwestern. I don't ever remember experiencing a fever. I take all my shots punctually as soon as I am reminded to be vaccinated. I

Some medicines can affect memory	systematically take all my medicines according to the doctor's instructions. I love being healthy at 82.5 years old, full of energy, and taking control of my health.

When I was about to finish this chapter involving memory, happiness, and joy, I received a video from my daughter. Rosita has not been able to leave Cuba; and, although technological developments have allowed us to see each other through my computer, I have not been able to hug and kiss her since I left Cuba on January 30, 1996.

The video deals with life and happiness. I thought that its inclusion in this chapter could add a more human approach to the book: It contains a sort of interview between life and her. Here it goes:

Rosita: Tell me Life "What do I have to do to make you last longer for many more years?"

Life: "Just use me."

Rosita "But everything that is used, disappears."

Life: "As a matter of one and at one doesn't use it, disappears anyway; therefore, use it without thinking about how much it will last; live without thinking about time, enjoy it because there is only one, and will disappear one day." A short silence takes place. "There are only moments of honey as well as moments of bitter lemon. Walk, don't run, enjoy the journey going through the blessings coming down from Heaven. Be thankful for being alive, strong enough to wait and to exist; but especially be humble to be grateful. Not every day does one need to be strong; sometimes one has to recognize weaknesses. Fight, stand up, be happy with what you have, and do not suffer because of what you don't have. Happiness cannot be prescribed as if it were a medicine at the pharmacy. Everybody makes it up in different circumstances. Do not delay writing your priorities because maybe you won't have time to polish your writing. Keep on learning from yourself one day after another because to learn is limitless. Finally, stop getting worried because thinking doesn't remove tomorrow's pains; as a matter of fact, it spoils today's happy moments. Life offers different ways to walk through, and to be alive is to enjoy it." Unknown author.

Food for thought:

1. This chapter is divided into systematic exercising, improving memory, the duo happiness and joy, and tenacity. Which one of these elements has impacted the readers' memories in a more conspicuous way?
2. After reading and meditating about the contents of this chapter, would they feel more motivated to introduce physical exercise into their daily lives in a systematic way?

Table des Matières